The Cabinetmaker & the Carver

Boston Furniture from Private Collections

Gerald W. R. Ward

Massachusetts Historical Society
Founded **1791**

Boston

2013

Distributed by
University of Virginia Press
Charlottesville

Published on the occasion of an exhibition
at the Massachusetts Historical Society,
October 4, 2013, through January 17, 2014.

"The Cabinet Maker and the Carver: Boston Furniture from Private Collections"
is part of Four Centuries of Massachusetts Furniture, a collaborative project of
the Massachusetts Historical Society and ten other institutions that features
exhibitions, lectures, demonstrations, and publications designed
to celebrate the Bay State's legacy of furniture making.

For more information, visit www.fourcenturies.org

Unless otherwise noted below, the photographs of the furniture in this book were taken by Laura Wulf
of Lightyears Photography, Jamaica Plain, Massachusetts.

Cat. no. 17: Photograph by Ray Fitzgerald.

Cat. no. 22: Photograph by David Bohl; Phillis Wheatley, lithograph by John B. Pendleton, ca. 1834, after engraving
by Scipio Moorhead, collections of the Massachusetts Historical Society.

Cat. no. 25: Photograph by Gavin Ashworth (courtesy of the Peabody Essex Museum).

Cat. no. 26: Playing cards made by Thomas Crehore of Dorchester, Mass., ca. 1820–1830, collections of the
Massachusetts Historical Society.

Cat. no. 27: George Archbald, daguerreotype, ca. 1840–1850, by an unidentified photographer,
collections of the Massachusetts Historical Society, Photo. 1.487.

Cat. no. 30b: Silhouettes of Louisa Catharine Adams and John Quincy Adams, by William James Hubbard, 1828,
private collection.

Cat. no. 31: Photograph by David Bohl (courtesy of Robert D. Mussey, Jr., and Clark Pearce).

Cat. no. 37: Invoice from Edward Hixon to the Massachusetts Historical Society, April 7, 1857, Massachusetts
Historical Society archives.

Cat. no. 39: Photograph by David Bohl.

Cat. no. 40: Photograph by Christopher Schuch.

On cover: desk and bookcase, cat. no. 20; page 4: detail of card table, cat. no. 21b; page 6: detail of desk, cat. no. 23a;
page 9: detail of desk, cat. no. 19; page 60: detail of side chair, cat. no. 23b; page 62: detail of library table, cat. no. 35;
page 64: back view of cane side chair, cat. no. 8.

Book design by Ondine Le Blanc, Massachusetts Historical Society

Acknowledgments

This exhibition would not have been possible without the generosity of our lenders, who granted us full access to their collections and graciously shared information about them. Although many have asked to remain anonymous, we are truly indebted to them all for letting us borrow their treasured objects for several months.

I am grateful to Dennis Fiori for the opportunity to work on this project and to the entire staff at the MHS for welcoming me into their fold as a guest. Anne Bentley has been of invaluable assistance at every step, as have Peter Drummey, Jayne Gordon, Carol Knauff, Mary Kearns, Peter Hood, and many others. Jim Connolly, Emilie Haertsch, and Ondine Le Blanc of the Publications Department have skillfully edited, designed, and produced this handsome publication.

Will Twombly of Spokeshave Designs is responsible for the exhibition's elegant design and installation. M-L Coolidge has ably acted as the project's registrar and field general. Laura Wulf has ably and cheerfully taken nearly all of the fine photographs in this catalogue, often working with M-L under challenging conditions on site. Early in the project, Caryne Eskridge, a student in the Winterthur Program, provided much-needed assistance.

As noted elsewhere, this publication and the events at the Massachusetts Historical Society are part of the Four Centuries of Massachusetts Furniture project, and our many colleagues involved in that collaborative effort have provided invaluable help, particularly Brock Jobe, its leader and driving force. Diane Garfield kept us on track with skill, patience, and good cheer, and every member of the steering committee was helpful at every turn.

Although I cannot name everyone who has been of assistance as this project came together, I would like to mention in particular Robert Mussey, Michael Wheeler, Ned Cooke, Jonathan Loring and The Seminarians, Clark Pearce, Seth Thayer, John and Marie VanderSande, Irfan Ali and William Coady, Jonathan Fairbanks, Nancy Carlisle, Carolyn Roy, Ronan Donohoe, Erik Gronning, Norman and Mary Gronning, Kem and Betsy Widmer, Tom Michie, Hilary Fairbanks and Timothy Burton, Don Friary, Toby Hall, Holly Izard, Holly Capozzi, Jane and Richard Nylander, Kelly H. L'Ecuyer, Nonie Gadsden, Dennis Carr, Nina Gray, Dean Lahikainen, Rob Emlen, Barbara and Ted Alfond, John and Marjorie McGraw, Selma Rutenburg, Ed and Cassandra Stone, Gerald Sheehan, Stephen Judge and James Skelton, Tara Cederholm, Martha S. Small, and Anne Bevan. And, as always in all that I do, I am indebted to Barbara McLean Ward for her enthusiastic support, editorial and scholarly skills, and patience.

Lenders to the Exhibition

The Colonial Society of Massachusetts
Mr. and Mrs. Francis L. Coolidge
Hilary Fairbanks and Timothy Burton
Norman and Mary Gronning
Stephen Judge and James Skelton
L. Knife & Son Corporate Collection
Massachusetts Historical Society
Mr. and Mrs. Edward L. Stone
Warner House Association

and several other anonymous private collections

Foreword

The Massachusetts Historical Society is pleased to present this exhibition as part of the Four Centuries of Massachusetts Furniture (FCMF) project, a collaborative effort of the Society and ten other institutions that features exhibitions, lectures, demonstrations, and publications designed to celebrate the Bay State's significant legacy of furniture making from the seventeenth century to the present. Our exhibition, which focuses tightly on Boston furniture from the late seventeenth century to about 1900, is designed to complement several other shows organized by our partner institutions that deal with furniture making in other parts of the state or from different time periods. Our show predominantly consists of exceptional objects from private local collections, giving the public an opportunity to view rarely seen works of great distinction. We are extremely grateful to our lenders, many of whom wish to remain anonymous, for generously sharing their precious objects with us and for supporting our efforts in many other ways.

The Society is pleased to have played a leading role in the extraordinary FCMF project, and I would like to take this opportunity to thank Brock Jobe of Winterthur, who has been the driving force behind our efforts, and all members of the FCMF steering committee. Diane Garfield, Project Administrator, also deserves a great deal of credit for her skilled handling of the many details that ground such a large undertaking. Many donors supported the FCMF initiative, and their gifts have made this exhibition and publication possible. A list included elsewhere in this catalogue recognizes their generosity.

For an institution more familiar with exhibiting paper-based material, an exhibition of this scale and this type of artifact presented many new challenges to the MHS staff, and they have responded brilliantly. Designer and fabricator Will Trombley has helped us transform our second-floor spaces into elegant galleries of beautiful furniture, accompanied by related documents, paintings, and other materials drawn from our own holdings. We are grateful to Gerry Ward, our guest curator, for his work in selecting the objects and preparing this publication. M-L Coolidge, the project's registrar, provided invaluable assistance with the many logistical issues that arise when photographing, shipping, and displaying such important objects within the confines of a tight timetable and limited budget. As always, Anne Bentley, MHS Curator of Art Collections, has worked closely with everyone involved to coordinate a lively, beautiful exhibition.

Furniture is indeed the thrust of this exhibition. But as you look at these extraordinary pieces, it is worth remembering that three-dimensional objects are also documents, albeit of a different sort. Even though they pique the interests of the antiquarian and excite the eye of the connoisseur, when examined carefully they can be no less revealing of the attitudes and values of their creators and owners than written words or printed type on paper—and thus are of value to the historian as well.

Dennis Fiori
President, Massachusetts
Historical Society

Introduction

What is the nature of Boston furniture? Searching for answers to that large question provided a framework for this small exhibition of Boston furniture from private collections ranging in date from about 1670 to 1900, covering in microcosm several centuries of a rich and varied furniture-making tradition. It is not a comprehensive framework—for example, relatively little space has been given to the work of John and Thomas Seymour, since Robert D. Mussey, Jr., has covered that ground so extensively in the recent past—but we have tried to present a range of works rarely seen in public that illustrate some of the characteristic forms of Boston furniture for more than two centuries. We have selected objects that, in many cases, vary from, and thus act as a supplement to, the Boston works on view in the Art of the Americas wing at the Museum of Fine Arts, Boston, a few blocks away on the Fenway. We also chose objects that reflect some of the current avenues of inquiry presented by scholars at the Winterthur Furniture Forum held in March 2013 and titled "New Perspectives on Boston Furniture, 1630–1860."

The thought that studying furniture can enhance our understanding of a community and its history has also been central to our purpose, for the objects produced in a given place, especially in the pre-industrial area, speak directly to the nature of that locale: to its ethnic origins, its economic conditions, its social attitudes and values, its state of technological development, its understanding of aesthetics, and other factors that define the shape and feel and look and status of a given place. It is not surprising, therefore, that Boston's furniture, like many of its citizens, speaks with a Boston accent. Or perhaps one should say several accents, for furniture represents both makers and users—people who often find themselves at different points of the socioeconomic structure—and over time, international influences have come from many different places around the globe. Depending on the object at hand, furniture thus can help us understand the conditions on the floor of a small shop or a large factory, as well as the genteel interiors of a colonial merchant's house or the more prosaic décor of an urban tenement in the nineteenth century.

Boston's importance as the home of a substantial furniture trade began in the mid seventeenth century and continued for more than two hundred years. Characterized by a strong reliance on English design and created within a sophisticated craft community featuring many specialized trades and immigrant craftsmen, Boston's colonial and federal furniture is particularly well known today. In the seventeenth century, Boston's joined and turned furniture was heavily indebted to London styles transplanted to the new world. Remarkably urbane furniture, embellished with exotic tropical hardwoods, was created here as early as the 1650s by the so-called Mason-Messenger-Edsall shops and others. This strong reliance on English design established a precedent that would last for centuries and is one of the hallmarks of Boston work.

As early as the seventeenth and early eighteenth centuries, Boston's craft structure featured a high degree of specialization, including turners, carvers, chairmakers, and other craftsmen with highly developed skills. As New England's largest town, Boston also was home to an important upholstery trade. Like silversmithing, which began in Boston in the 1650s with the firm of John Hull and Robert Sanderson, upholstery made use of expensive materials that only the wealthiest consumers could afford. A sophisticated and hierarchical craft structure, dating to the earliest days, is another defining characteristic of the Boston furniture trade.

"Immigrants and imports" are two more characteristics that define Boston (and other colonial) furniture. Boston was the closest of any city in the original thirteen colonies to England. At first of necessity but continuing with each generation, Boston's furniture was indebted to a significant number of immigrant craftsmen who came in wave after wave, bringing with them technological skills and an up-to-date design sense that they had learned abroad and in turn infused into the Boston market. The same active international connections that transported these craftsmen also brought to Boston many fine English objects that served as prototypes for local designs. That network and also, starting perhaps as early as 1650, brought rosewood, snakewood, cedrela, mahogany, and other cabinetmaking woods from the West Indies and South America that would enrich the vocabulary of cabinet woods.

A new Massachusetts charter in 1691 resulted in an influx of royal officials and administrators who helped bring a new style and a new technology to Boston, one way in which politics affected the course of decorative arts. The source of that style, today called the early baroque or the William and Mary style, can be traced to the courtly modes of France. Its forms were transmitted through England and Holland to America. It featured greater verticality and delicacy than its seventeenth-century counterparts, and it often reflected an interest in shimmering optical effects and highly ornamented passages, including elegant turnings, rich carving, inlay, and japanning. Case furniture, with dovetailed pine carcasses and drawer fronts veneered with burl maple or walnut, was made by craftsmen who termed themselves "cabinetmakers" rather than "joiners."

These cabinetmakers, many of them immigrants seeking greater economic opportunity, introduced elegant Georgian styles in the early eighteenth century, at the height of Boston's colonial prosperity, a time when the city's numerous woodworkers produced one of the most significant bodies of work created in the colonies. Among the eighteenth-century styles favored locally were japanned objects of various types, as well as blockfront and bombé (or "swelled") case pieces. Japanning, done in imitation of true Asian lacquer, was another largely urban craft, and it had significant appeal to Bostonians, establishing a local fascination with the Far East that has remained for centuries. Blockfront case pieces—baroque objects with an undulating façade of convex sides flanking a concave center—were probably derived from Continental sources but also struck a responsive chord locally. From the 1730s forward, Boston blockfront furniture stands as one of the most distinctive and elegant expressions of colonial American furniture.

The rococo ornamental style of the mid eighteenth century emphasized substantial furniture often embellished with carving featuring C-scrolls, claw-and-ball feet, and pierced splats, along with Gothic, Chinese, and natural motifs such as rocks, shells, and leafage, and occasional touches of asymmetry. Boston makers (and some from Essex County) such as George Bright and John Cogswell produced impressive and expensive case furniture in the distinctive bombé mode, and carvers such

as John Welch and others employed their talents on forms from picture frames to chairs, as well as on ships and buildings. Although rococo elements are present in their furniture, Bostonians embraced this fanciful, ultimately French, style cautiously, with a characteristic blend of frugality and conservative restraint—two of the more persistent traits of Boston work. Bostonians rarely dive in when dipping a toe will suffice.

In furniture, as in other areas, Boston was the center of New England. This centrality had several important consequences. Many craftsmen, for example, came to Boston to be trained and ultimately returned home, carrying design sensibilities with them. Some Bostonians, such as Nathaniel Gould, were trained locally but then left to pursue careers elsewhere. In Gould's case, he left for Salem, where he dominated the local furniture trade for several decades. The size of the Boston woodworking trades also meant that production could exceed local demand, and a vigorous export trade flourished in Boston for many years, sending objects to other parts of coastal America, to Canada, and to the West Indies. The existence of this export trade has caused problems for modern connoisseurs, some of whom are engaged in a debate as to whether (for example) some important eighteenth-century chairs were made in Boston or in New York (where many have been found) or even in Rhode Island.

As in other colonies, the onset of Revolutionary activities, beginning locally roughly with the blockade of Boston in 1773, curtailed the activities of American craftsmen of all kinds until the end of hostilities a decade later. Many great Boston objects must have been lost to vandalism and fires in this turbulent era, while other fine examples were taken by wealthy Loyalists to Canada and England. Although Massachusetts led the way in rebelling against and then defeating the British in the American Revolution, Massachusetts patrons and craftsmen remained as wedded to English taste after the Revolution as they were before it. English designs were again transmitted by immigrant craftsmen and imported objects, and that communication was also augmented by widely disseminated English pattern books of George Hepplewhite, Thomas Sheraton, and others.

After the war, more immigrant English craftsmen, principally John and Thomas Seymour, who arrived in Boston in 1793, continued to make furniture heavily indebted to English prototypes, including mahogany sideboards, tambour desks, a variety of seating, and other forms. Although the Seymours have been well known, they were not working alone in Boston at this time, as the town's expansion supported many fine woodworkers, including Stephen Badlam, Benjamin Frothingham, and the Skillin family of carvers. Specialization continued to characterize the Boston craft system, with talented artisans such as the carver Thomas Wightman, ornamental painter John Ritto Penniman, and gilder and looking-glass maker John Doggett playing significant roles.

As the nineteenth century progressed, heavier, more archaeologically correct furniture in the antique style, echoing more literally the designs of ancient Greece, Rome, and occasionally Egypt, was produced by Boston firms such as Isaac Vose and Son and Emmons and Archbald in the 1820s and 1830s. These were large shops when compared to their eighteenth-century forebears, employing ten or a dozen journeymen and apprentices and maintaining a commodious warehouse for the sale of goods. Boston produced a wide variety of forms in this period, including many elegant forms of chairs and other seating furniture.

Boston was also home to many mid nineteenth-century furniture firms that, in a spirit of vibrant eclecticism, created objects in the Gothic, Elizabethan, rococo, Renaissance, and other successive and overlapping revival styles. In addition, several local makers specialized in innovative patent furniture as the century moved on, often creating objects with multiple functions. French taste increased in popularity in this period, and Augustus Eliaers was one of its leading proponents. Trained in France, Eliaers had a successful career in Boston in the 1850s and 1860s before he returned to his native country.

Improved transportation and communication networks in the nineteenth century began to blur the regional aesthetic and distinctive accent that had characterized Boston furniture for about two centuries. Many individuals who made furniture at this time also imported objects from other cities—New York, for example—to sell at retail in their "warerooms" or "show rooms." Occasionally, they would add their own label to the imported pieces, making life difficult for furniture scholars today.

The great fire of 1872 and other factors combined to curtail Boston's furniture industry after about 1880. In the last quarter of the nineteenth century, a reaction against the heavily ornamented, often factory-made furniture widely available at the time caused some people to seek simpler forms that were more expressive of the handcrafted furniture of pre-industrial times. Furniture made during this arts and crafts movement reflected not a single style but rather a theory of design that reunited the hand and eye of the maker. The Society of Arts and Crafts, Boston, incorporated in 1897, was established

to bring Designers and Workmen into mutually helpful relations, and to encourage workmen to execute designs of their own. It endeavors to stimulate in workmen an appreciation of the dignity and the value of good design; to counteract the popular impatience of Law and Form, and the desire for over ornamentation and specious originality. It will insist upon the necessity of sobriety and restraint, of ordered arrangement, of due regard for the relation between the form of its object and its use, and of harmony and fitness in the decorations put upon it.

In Boston, where an interest in history has always been strong, objects made in a colonial revival style were a substantial component of this movement. Furniture designed by H. H. Richardson and Francis H. Bacon, woodwork carved by Johannes Kirchmayer, and objects produced by A. H. Davenport and Irving and Casson are among the more well-known objects of this period—indeed, the latter two firms received significant national commissions.

Large local firms, such as Paine's Furniture, made and retailed objects on a more vernacular level and dominated the middle-class market. Although the Paine name is well known today, this type of furniture is largely below the level of historical scrutiny exercised by art museums. It remains little studied and collected, although it formed a massive part of the market. Furniture making in Boston in the twenty-first century is not a robust industry, and most furniture is brought to customers through large retail operations that sell objects made in North Carolina, China, or elsewhere. Fortunately, a community of studio artists, working in both innovative and traditional styles or a blend of the two, maintains the small-shop tradition started by Mason and Messenger in the 1650s, and the robust North Bennet Street School keeps woodworking craftsmanship alive through its courses and programs.

Central to this exhibition's purpose is the concept that furniture is an important type of three-dimensional historical evidence, often as revealing (when interpreted) as the written word. Furniture tells us much about the past—about social customs and human interaction, about the relationship between Americans and the world, about the changing nature of technology and the evolution of aesthetics, among many other topics. By providing a snapshot of Boston's distinctive furniture tradition, this exhibition, we believe, provides another lens through which to examine the city's long and distinguished history.

Joined cupboard with drawers 1

Attributed to to the Harvard College Joiners
Cambridge, Mass., 1670-1690
Oak, maple, cedar, pine
H. 51 7/8 in., W. 45 7/8 in., D. 20 1/2 in.
Private collection

The furniture scholar Robert F. Trent has linked this cupboard with a group of related examples attributed to three generations of Harvard College joiners, so-called, who worked in Cambridge and created furniture closely related to that produced in nearby Boston. This cupboard, in the applied ornament style, is distinguished by its three drawers in the lower section, an unusual variation in the composition of these large objects, which typically provided a focal point in the 17th-century interior. Although they offered relatively little storage space given their bulk—and awkward space at that—they demonstrated the owner's taste and wealth, and they also provided flat surfaces for the display of silver, ceramics, glass, and other family treasures.

The cupboard is also associated with more recent generations of New England furniture enthusiasts. It is stamped five times with the name "D. T. WARD" in a type of early 19th-century brand that often represents the name of a later owner. In the 20th century, it was acquired by the illustrious firm of Israel Sack on Charles Street in Boston. Sack's firm, which eventually moved to New York and was carried on until fairly recently by his three sons, became one of the most reputable and long-lasting dealers in early American furniture. The notable New England collector Dwight Blaney (1865–1944) purchased the piece from Sack in 1918. Blaney, a genteel artist and fisherman, among other things, was also a founder of the Walpole Society, an early and ongoing distinguished group of Americana collectors.

2 Turned great chair

Boston or Charlestown, Mass., ca. 1670–1700
Poplar
H. 46 1/4 in., W. 24 3/4 in., D. 18 1/4 in.
Private collection

Several features, identified by the furniture historian Benno M. Forman, suggest that this impressive slat-back chair was made in the late 17th century in Boston or Charlestown. Among the salient characteristics pointing to this attribution are its flat draw-shaven arms, the three back slats, the well-articulated finials, and the use of poplar (*Populus* spp.) for the principal posts. In addition, many chairs of this type, like this example, were colored black originally.

Forman suggested that Nathaniel Adams, Edmund Larkin, and Stephen Fosdick were among the possible makers of these Boston/Charlestown chairs. Closely related versions were also made in Salem, but with maple posts and slightly different finials. Samuel Beadle, a turner trained in Charlestown, went there in the 1660s and may have transferred the style to that town.

Despite the scholarly detective work by Forman and others, the maker of this armchair remains uncertain, reflecting the difficult task of linking surviving objects with specific artisans in the face of scant documentation. It nevertheless stands as an important survivor of one type of Boston's earliest seating furniture, evocative of the bold stance, sturdy nature, and substantial proportions of the first flowerings of Boston furniture making.

Turned great chair 3

Boston or Charlestown, Mass., ca. 1675-1700
Maple, ash
H. 45 in., W. 23 3/4 in., D. 17 3/8 in.
Massachusetts Historical Society

The turned finials of this imposing armchair relate to those found on other spindle-back examples, some with Boston histories, and it is likely that it was made in Boston or Charlestown in the later part of the 17th century. Although one finial and one handhold have been replaced, it remains in good condition.

When this chair was given to the Society in 1930 by the heirs of Mary Edson Cushing, it came with a history of having been the "library chair" of Mather Byles (1706/7–1788), a colorful Boston minister, poet, and author.

And so it might have been, although given the age of the chair, Byles probably inherited it from his maternal grandfather, Increase Mather (1639–1723), or his uncle Cotton Mather (1663–1728). Byles also inherited many of his books from those worthy divines. With a comfortable cushion, or squab, placed upon its seat, this magisterial chair was a fitting throne for several generations of Boston's distinguished clergymen.

4 Desk box

Attributed to the Mason-Messenger shop tradition
Boston, Mass., 1670-1710
Oak, walnut
H. 11 in., W. 24 3/4 in., D. 19 1/2 in.
Private collection

This small box, a form that rarely survives from 17th-century Boston, testifies to the importance of literacy and commerce in the Massachusetts Bay Colony. Although it lacks an early history, the profile of its base molding matches that found on large case pieces attributed to the Mason-Messenger shop tradition, suggesting that it may have been made using the same molding plane.

The hinged lid opens to reveal a modest interior with two shelves running from side to side at the rear, each divided initially by vertical partitions into smaller compartments. The front section of the interior could have held books, a ledger, or larger items. The desk shows great evidence of use, including the inevitable ink stains, and it bears the initials "RH" scratched on the back, probably for an early owner. Hinged at the top, the slant lid provides a surface for writing or for propping up a book for reading, giving rise to the term "writing slope" often used to describe the form. The small flat surface at the top of the box, above the lid, might have held an inkwell, writing implements, a candlestick, or other small articles.

Here, the slant lid is simply of oak, although in more elaborate examples the writing surface would have been covered in leather or fabric. Such portable desk boxes would have been placed on top of a table or other flat surface when needed for reading or writing.

Attributed to the Mason-Messenger shop tradition,
with turnings attributed to the Edsall shop tradition
Boston, Mass., ca. 1660-1680
Oak, pine, walnut, lignum vitae
H. 16 1/2 in., W. 18 in., D. 8 1/2 in.
Private collection

A rare survivor, this small cabinet (or case of boxes) demonstrates nearly the full range of ornament of the period in miniature form. Only a few New England examples associated with the Mason-Messenger shop of Boston (see also cat. no. 6) and the Symonds family shops of Salem are known, some dated in the late 1670s. They are notable for their architectonic fronts, embellished with complex moldings and occasionally, as here, with crisply turned applied-split spindles and bosses. The ornaments here are in a pattern often attributed to the shop tradition started by Thomas Edsall (1588–1676), a London-trained immigrant turner.

Used in wealthy homes, cabinets like this offered a degree of organized space not typically found in 17th-century case furniture: the interior here houses seven small drawers, some of which appear to be fitted with lignum vitae pulls. Randle Holme, in his *Academie or Storehouse of Armory and Blazon* (London, 1682), noted "this kind of cabinette is such as Ladyes keepe their rings, necklaces, Braceletts and Jewlls In." They could also serve as repositories for coins, writing materials, and other small objects, and they were designed to be transportable, allowing a family to save a few possessions while fleeing a fire or other household disaster.

Some of the Salem examples bear the initials of their original owners, although this cabinet lacks any such carving. This cabinet also shows no evidence of the small turned feet that are found on the handful of other surviving examples.

6 Joined chest of drawers

Attributed to the Mason-Messenger shop tradition
Boston, Mass., ca. 1690
Oak, pine, cedar, rosewood
H. 35 3/4 in., W. 38 7/8 in., D. 29 1/2 in.
Private collection

Remarkably, within only a few decades of its founding in 1630 Boston could support silversmiths, joiners, turners, and other craftsmen creating significant objects in reasonably up-to-date English styles, representative of the Puritans' desire and ability to replicate some aspects of their life in England in the new world.

In furniture, the English-trained joiners Ralph Mason (1599–1678/9) and Henry Messenger (d. 1681) established at midcentury a Boston shop tradition that extended for several generations. Today the most stylish furniture associated with 17th-century Boston is often attributed to this lineage of skilled artisans (see also cat. nos. 4–5). Their work, at its most ambitious level, has been said to reflect the international artistic movement known as Anglo-Netherlandish Mannerism

or, alternatively, to be more in a late Renaissance style that lacks the exaggeration, wit, and irony of the more extreme Mannerist work. In any event, their furniture is well conceived, displays a knowledge of classical architectural proportions and ornament, and demonstrates great skill in technique.

This chest of drawers is fashioned in two cases, perhaps to facilitate transporting the piece and navigating the cramped stairway in a 17th-century house. Here, the upper section contains two small drawers in line over a deep single drawer, while the lower section contains two case-wide drawers of equal size. The turned front feet may be original; the rear feet are formed by extensions of the stiles. The plaques of veneer on the drawer fronts and front stiles are probably rosewood (*Dalbergia* spp.), one of several tropical hard-

woods imported into Boston at this early date and used for ornamental purposes on the finest furniture.

This type of "Pilgrim Century" furniture has been collected now for well more than a century. A pencil inscription on the underside of the top, dated April 1877, indicates that this chest, then "250 years old," was sold by John Allen, an early Boston dealer and collector, adding a layer of interest to the long life of this extraordinary object. A John Allen, presumably the same man, lent a number of relics associated with George Washington, John Quincy Adams, the Marquis de Lafayette, and others to the exhibition of Revolutionary relics organized at 56 Beacon Street by the Ladies' Centennial Commission in June 1875.

Japanned high chest of drawers **7**
Boston, Mass., ca. 1710-1720
Maple, pine
H. 63 in., W. 42 1/2 in., D. 22 1/8 in.
Private collection

"Japanning" was most popular, in colonial America, in Boston. Used to enliven the façades of dressing tables, high chests, and tall clocks, this evocation of true Asian lacquer was accomplished in the colonies through the use of gesso and paint. The japanner created slightly raised exotic images of animals, buildings, birds, and other exotica usually set against a black or tortoiseshell background.

This high chest of drawers in the early baroque style, although its vibrancy has been muted by time, was originally a bright, colorful example, and it is also notable for its elegantly turned trumpet-shaped legs. Its drawer fronts contain many charming *chinoiserie* elements, and the case sides are decorated with larger images. The art historian Ethan Lasser has suggested that these decorative schemes, rather than being randomly applied ornaments simply derived from pattern books or other sources, can on occasion represent actual narratives of sea voyages, with depictions of locations and shorelines that could be read by a masculine mercantile audience in the 18th century.

A substantial number of japanned pieces are inscribed on their interiors or backs with various names. This example is inscribed "Bayley" several times, probably indicating an early owner; a craftsman of that name has not yet been identified.

8 Cane side chair

Boston, Mass., ca. 1690-1705
Beech, cane
H. 52 1/2 in., W. 18 in., D. 19 1/4 in.
Massachusetts Historical Society

Cane chairs were made in large quantities in London, generated by an industry in which craft specialization played a significant part, utilizing an early form of interchangeable parts to increase the volume of production. They were exported in significant numbers to colonial America. This chair and its mate in the Winterthur Museum collection, however, are important early examples of cane chairmaking in colonial Boston. The Winterthur chair is made of American beech (*Fagus grandifloria*), as determined by microanalysis, suggesting an American origin, and the MHS chair has a Winthrop family history, helping to pinpoint Boston as the likely place of origin.

Determining the maker of these early chairs has involved much speculation, even though both bear the initials of an as-yet-unidentified craftsman. Benno M. Forman has suggested that they are the work of an English-trained immigrant turner (rather than a cane-chairmaker specifically) working in Boston. The MHS chair may have originally belonged to Waitstill Winthrop (1642–1717), a notable Boston jurist who, Forman speculates, might have ordered his fashionable furniture from John Brocas (d. 1740). Brocas, a cabinetmaker trained in England, arrived in Boston as early as 1696, presumably bringing with him the new early baroque style. Brocas, in turn, may have jobbed out the chair commission to another local craftsman.

Side chair **9a**
Boston, Mass., ca. 1720–1730
Maple, cane
H. 44 1/2 in., W. 17 1/2 in., D. 16 3/4 in.
Private collection

Side chair **9b**
Boston, Mass., ca. 1720–1730
Maple, cane
H. 45 1/4 in., W. 18 1/2 in., D. 19 1/2 in.
Private collection

The making of cane chairs was an urban craft in which Boston makers dominated the New England market for several generations (see also cat. no. 8). These two chairs—similar but with subtle differences—represent the vitality of the Boston chairmaking industry in the early 18th century. Each demonstrates the basic vocabulary of the style: a carved and scrolled crest rail, a caned back and seat, and a shaped skirt outlined with molding. The principal difference between them is the shape of the front legs: the ebonized example (9b) has turned legs ending in so-called Spanish (or brush) feet, while the other chair (9a) has squarish cabriole (or crook) legs. The ebonized chair has a bold ball-and-ring front stretcher, while the second chair's stretcher is a more subtle ball-and-reel form, and there are also variations in the arrangement and configuration of their side stretchers.

One chair (9a) is also marked with a large punched capital "I" with a cross-serif on the back of the lower seat rail. It is one of more than two dozen surviving chairs with this mark, thought to be that of an unidentified craftsman. The "I" group chairs show considerable variation in their carving, in the design of their stretchers, and in other details, but the preponderance of the evidence suggests that they were all made in Boston.

10 Banister-back armchair

Boston, Mass., ca. 1710-1740

Maple, ash, rush

H. 53 in., W. 24 1/4 in., D. 24 3/4 in.

Collection of Norman and Mary Gronning

This majestic armchair represents one of the high points in Boston seating furniture of the early 18th century. Distinguished by its elegant turnings, scrolled arms and handholds, architectonic banisters (or balusters) in the back, and carved crest, the armchair has a bold stance and commanding presence that serve as reminders of the power and prestige it conveyed by association to the person using it.

Similar chairs were made elsewhere in eastern Massachusetts and in Portsmouth, New Hampshire, but this example exhibits the characteristics typical of Boston work, including the specific configuration of the columnar turned stiles, the urn-shaped finials, the pattern of leafage and C-scrolls in the crest rail, and the carved front stretcher. It shares several design features with leather chairs produced contemporaneously in Boston, probably in the same shops, including the use of rectangular side and rear stretchers.

Boston, Mass., ca. 1725-1740
Maple, original leather upholstery
H. 43 3/4 in., W. 18 1/2 in., D. 19 1/4 in.
Collection of Norman and Mary Gronning

The "Boston chair," as the general type was known in the period, was made in massive quantities (by pre-industrial standards) by several Boston shops during the second quarter of the 18th century, an era of great prosperity in the town. Similar chairs were also made in Salem and in Portsmouth, New Hampshire, and many of these New England chairs were shipped to Philadelphia, New York, and other locations up and down the East Coast and to the West Indies as part of the region's substantial export trade. This example, remarkably, retains its original Russia-leather covering, secured with double rows of brass nails, a less expensive treatment than cloth or cane. The chair's shaped back, called "crook'd" at the time, provided the sitter with a modicum of comfort that foreshadowed a growing emphasis on good ergonomics that would come to typify 18th-century furniture. The account book of Boston upholsterer Thomas Fitch reveals that he sold "crook'd back chairs" for 27 shillings each in 1722/3, thought to represent the approximate introduction of this specific form to Boston chairmaking.

12 Chest-on-chest with secretary drawer

Boston, Mass., ca. 1730
Walnut, walnut veneer, white pine
H. 80 1/4 in., W. 41 1/2 in., D. 22 1/4 in.
Warner House Association; gift of Mrs. Arthur D. Hill (1962.1)

This large object—essentially a chest-on-chest with glazed doors in the upper case and a secretary (or writing) drawer in the lower—is one of a few surviving examples of Boston furniture in what Edward S. Cooke, Jr., and scholars have termed an early Georgian style. Distinguished by its stately double-domed upper case, carefully selected walnut veneers, and inlaid decoration in the pediment drawers, this object closely follows English design prototypes and may well have been made by an immigrant cabinetmaker trained in England. As with the nearly contemporaneous silver made by John Coney, Edward Winslow, and other goldsmiths in Boston, this chest-on-chest's elegance is testimony to the prosperity that Boston had achieved only a century after initial settlement, as well as the desire of its citizens to see themselves as part of an Anglo-American Atlantic community.

Bureau dressing table **13**
Boston, Mass., 1730-1740
Mahogany, white pine
H. 29 3/4 in., W. 35 in., D. 21 in.
Private collection

The blockfront façade, in which the case sides project and the center is recessed, is one of the signatures of Boston 18th-century case furniture, seen on several examples in this exhibition. This bureau dressing table is one of the earliest manifestations of the design in Boston, and it is also notable for its architectural front, framed by four fluted pilasters topped with Doric capitals. The four turned front feet—in all likelihood original—are an unusual element found on only a few other Boston case pieces of this period. Although the maker's name is not known, it has been suggested that the bureau table was likely the work of a London-trained immigrant craftsman such as William Price (1684–1771). Possibly made originally for William (d. 1781) and Elizabeth Parker of Portsmouth, New Hampshire, the dressing table descended to their son Bishop Samuel Parker (1744–1804) of Boston and, in turn, to later family members. This exquisite bureau table may have been one of the furnishings that contributed to Parker's somewhat grandiose style of life, which one colleague noted went "rather beyond what is merely decent and necessary."

**14
a**
Side chair
Boston, Mass., 1735-1745
Walnut, maple
H. 41 in., W. 22 ³/₈ in., D. 22 in.
Private collection

**14
b**
Backstool
Boston, Mass., ca. 1730-1745
Walnut, maple
H. 40 ³/₄ in., W. 21 ¹/₂ in., D. 24 in.
Private collection

Graceful curves tracing elegant lines predominate in seating furniture of the late baroque (or Queen Anne) style. This leather-upholstered backstool (14b), with cabriole legs at both front and rear and with flat stretchers, is one of only three known Boston examples. Occasionally made en suite with easy chairs, backstools were sometimes also known as "dressing chairs" and may have been used in bedchambers.

Graceful American side chairs with "hoop" shoulders of this type (14a), horseshoe-shaped seats, and flat stretchers were long attributed to Newport, Rhode Island, but more recent research by Leigh Keno and his collabora-

tors has suggested that they are of Boston manufacture. As noted by furniture historian Nancy Goyne Evans, these chairs provide evidence of the many international design sources that cumatively affected the look of 18th-century Boston furniture. Although most closely related to English prototypes, the chair reveals the impact of Chinese forms in the profile of its vase-shaped splat and cabriole legs, but these designs can also be traced to classical antiquity and to the 17th-century baroque mode of continental Europe. It has a history in the Cutts-Gerrish families of Kittery, Maine.

One of a small group of distinctive Boston-area dressing tables with flat- and round-blocked façades, this example is distinguished by its small claw-and-ball feet and excellent condition. Significantly, it has a history in the Lee family of Cambridge through several generations. The original owner may have been Judge Joseph Lee (1710/1–1802) of Cambridge, described as "one of the most disorderly members of a quiet class" at Harvard. He acquired what is now the Hooper-Lee-Nichols house at 159 Brattle Street in 1758. Something of a half-hearted Tory, Lee left town during the Revolution, but he returned after the war and lived out his life in Cambridge.

Although most of the other tables in this group lack histories, a related example at Winterthur came down in the Cushing family of Boston merchants. That history, when coupled with this Lee family piece, helps tie the group to the shop of an as-yet-unidentified Boston cabinetmaker. A notable feature of the group is their use of large imported English brasses attached to the fixed lower front rail in a marvelously nonfunctional manner. This example also has six small drawers in two tiers.

16 Chest of drawers

The Netherlands, ca. 1725-1750
Walnut, oak
H. 33 3/4 in., W. 35 7/8 in., D. 23 3/4 in.
Private collection

Boston's blockfront furniture (see cat. nos. 13, 15, 19) is a distinctive contribution to furniture of the 18th century, used from the 1730s until the end of the century. Hundreds of examples have survived, a testimony to the popularity of the form. Widely used in Massachusetts and to equal aesthetic success in Newport, Rhode Island, and in Connecticut, the design is a hallmark of early New England cabinetmaking. Yet its precise origin in Anglo-European furniture, from which most American designs emanate, has long puzzled scholars. Undulating façades with some relationship to Boston blocking are seen in

English, French, German, Spanish, and Cuban furniture of the period, but rarely is the relationship with American work as strongly evident as it is with the Dutch chest of drawers exhibiting rounded blocking. Although it may not be a direct prototype for American work, the intriguing relationship between this Dutch piece and its Boston counterparts is an important reminder that Boston furniture needs to be studied in an international context that embraces the complex interconnectivity of the 18th-century world of design.

Desk and bookcase 17
Boston, Mass., 1740-1750
Walnut, walnut veneer, white pine
H. 90 in., W. 38 in., D. 22 in.
Private collection

The monumental desk and bookcase is a signature form of Boston mid-18th-century furniture. Like a modern computer, these objects provided a new level of specialization and organization that was unheard of just a generation or two earlier. Their numerous small drawers, pigeonholes, and compartments provided as many as 60 or more discrete areas for the storage of ledgers, correspondence, and documents. Often containing hidden (or "secret") compartments—this example includes six such spaces—these objects provided an efficient and secure working environment for Boston's merchants, many of whom were energetically engaged in the international Atlantic trading network. Moreover, these desk and bookcases were also often outstanding examples of the cabinetmaker's art. Described by the furniture historian John T. Kirk as "starkly elegant," this early iteration of the form is notable for its inlaid compass-work stars (a Boston feature), richly articulated interiors in both cases, and glorious inlaid fans in recessed shells in the tympanum.

18 Desk

Boston, Mass., ca. 1765–1770
Mahogany, white pine
H. 44 1/4 in., W. 37 7/8 in., D. 25 1/2 in.
Private collection

This desk, owned originally by Stephen Salisbury I (1746–1829), is one of a small group of pieces that vary from the typical slant-front type and were specifically designed to fulfill the needs of an active 18th-century merchant. Salisbury may have brought it with him when he went from Boston to Worcester in 1767 to open a branch office of the hardware and import business he operated with his older brother, Samuel, and he used it in his magnificent Worcester home, built in 1772. After his death, his much-younger widow, Elizabeth, remodeled parts of the house, and at that time the desk may have been given to her nephew Edward Tuckerman IV (1817–1886). It has descended in the family to the present owner. Related examples include ones owned originally by John Amory, Peter Oliver, and Thomas Hancock, whose massive desk is perhaps the *ne plus ultra* of the form.

Designed to be used while standing, the Salisbury desk has a sloping writing surface hinged to the case. The top two drawer fronts are false, and the lid lifts to reveal a compartment with nine pigeonholes, two drawers, and a space for a ledger. Stylish elements, including its rounded façade, acanthus-carved drop, carved knees and brackets, and claw-and-ball feet, make this desk as aesthetically pleasing as it is useful.

Desk **19**

Probably carved by John Welch
Boston, Mass., 1755–1785
Mahogany, white pine
H. 44 3/4 in., W. 44 3/4 in., D. 22 1/2 in.
Private collection

The slant-front desk is a landmark form of Boston 18th-century furniture, seemingly made in substantial quantities for the town's merchants (see cat. no. 18), ministers, and others in need of a highly functional as well as ornamental work station. This blockfront example, however, rises above the ordinary iteration of the form for two reasons. It has a long history in the family of the current owner, and a handwritten genealogy preserved with the desk suggests that it may have been made for Henry Quincy (1727–1780) of Quincy, Massachusetts. Moreover, its four claw-and-ball feet are embellished with delightful carved faces (see p. 9), a detail rarely seen on Boston furniture of this period. These faces have been attributed to the hand of John Welch (1711–1789), the renowned carver of some of John Singleton Copley's picture frames, of woodwork in the Old State House, and at least some of the town's finest

rococo-style furniture (see also cat. no. 20). It is possible that these faces, similar to those carved on two objects in the Museum of Fine Arts, Boston, were meant to represent the ancient forest symbol of the green man.

20 Desk and bookcase

Carving attributed to John Welch
Boston, Mass., ca. 1750-1755
Mahogany, eastern white pine, ash
H. 94 1/4 in., W. 41 7/8 in., D. 22 7/8 in.
Private collection

In 1993, in the inaugural edition of the annual journal *American Furniture*, Alan Miller identified a substantial group of high-style Boston mid-18th-century furniture that he attributed to the shop of an as-yet-unidentified cabinetmaker. In Miller's analysis, this shop's output is "not urban British furniture made in the colonies; it is Boston furniture informed and transformed by the grandeur of European styles." As such it suggests a sophisticated English background or period of advanced training by the shop's master, an ongoing theme in Boston's Anglophilic furniture.

This imposing desk and bookcase is a significant member of that shop tradition. It was owned originally by the wealthy Loyalist merchant Gilbert Deblois (1725–1791) and his wife, Ann Coffin, who were married in 1749 and who also owned an important Boston clothespress now in the collection of the Museum of Fine Arts, Boston. In the inventory of Deblois's worldly goods taken after his death, this desk and bookcase was valued at nine pounds, only equaled in value by a tall-case clock (now in the collection of the Chipstone Foundation). As with many other objects attributed to this shop, the carving at its base and pediment is attributed to John Welch (1711–1789), one of Boston's premier carvers (see also cat. nos. 19, 21b). The desk descended through several generations of the Deblois family until it burst upon the auction market in 2007.

Card table
Possibly carved by John Welch
Boston, Mass., ca. 1760
Mahogany, white pine
H. 28 1/4 in., W. 34 in., D. 16 1/2 in. (closed)
Private collection

As the 18th century progressed, a relaxation in thought and behavior made it more acceptable for Bostonians to indulge in such frivolous activities as card playing (and its concomitant gambling), previously considered beyond the pale. Although almost any flat surface would suffice, specialized furniture forms were produced for gaming in fashionable, wealthy homes. These two turret-cornered card tables are among the finest Boston examples from this period. With the table open, the rounded corners could be used to hold candlesticks, while the shallow recesses in the top held each player's fiche (or chips). One (cat. no. 21a) is notable for its combination of claw-and-ball carved front feet and pad rear feet with vertical veining, and it retains its original aubergine tooled-leather playing surface. By tradition, it was owned originally by a minister: Rev. John Howland (1721–1804), who was a pastor in Plympton, Massachusetts, from 1746 until his death.

Card table **21**
b
Possibly carved by John Welch
Boston, Mass., ca. 1760
Mahogany, white pine, maple
H. 27 7/8 in., W. 34 1/8 in., D. 14 5/8 in. (closed)
Private collection

The second table (cat. no. 21b) has unusual hairy paw front feet, and its knees are carved with a fantastic animal mask (see p. #), a rarity in Boston furniture only seen on one other surviving example. The carving on each table has in recent years been attributed to Boston's most notable carver of the period, John Welch (1711–1789). Born and trained in Boston, Welch was one of the few American craftsmen who traveled abroad. He visited England in the late 1750s and may have been exposed to the latest English designs before his return to Boston about 1760.

22 Card table

Boston, Mass., 1760–1770
Mahogany, pine
H. 28 1/2 in., W. 35 3/4 in., D. 15 1/4 in. (closed)
Massachusetts Historical Society

Phillis Wheatley.

Pendleton's Lithog.ᵞ Boston.

By tradition, this card table was owned by John and Susannah Wheatley of Boston and was used by their servant Phillis as her writing desk, and that association with America's first African American poet lifts it above the ordinary. In 1761 John purchased Phillis (ca. 1754–1784), an enslaved person who had been kidnapped in West Africa, as a servant for his wife. The Wheatley family soon recognized Phillis's abilities and encouraged her to learn English and to read widely in religion and the Western classics. By 1767 she had published her verse, and in 1773 her *Poems on Various Subjects* appeared to national and international acclaim and she was freed by John Wheatley. The frontispiece to her book was engraved by Scipio Moorhead, an enslaved African of Boston in service to a neighbor and friend of the Wheatleys, Rev. John Moorhead of the Church of the Presbyterian Strangers. Scipio chose to depict Phillis at work, seated in a late baroque side chair with quill in hand and writing on an oval surface, perhaps a stylized rendition of the top of this card table. In addition to its historic significance, Phillis's table, with its undulating front skirt and boldly carved claw-and-ball feet, is a superb example of Boston craftsmanship in the rococo style.

Card table **23 a**
Possibly by James Graham
Boston, Mass., 1760-1785
Mahogany, maple, pine
H. 28 1/4 in., W. 35 1/2 in., D. 17 1/2 in.
(closed)
Private collection

Side chair **23 b**
Possibly by James Graham
Boston, Mass., 1760-1785
Mahogany, oak, soft maple
H. 38 1/4 in., W. 24 5/8 in., D. 18 7/8 in.
Private collection

The extraordinary carving on these two major pieces of Boston rococo furniture has been linked to the hand of a highly skilled cabinetmaker and carver who was responsible for much of the finest Boston furniture of the period. Kemble Widmer II has suggested recently that James Graham (1728–1808), a Scottish immigrant who arrived in Boston in 1754, may have been the craftsman who created this amazing body of work. Graham's distinctive carving hand (if it is indeed his) is often found on chairs, but few are as well developed or elaborate as this high-style side chair owned in the 18th century by the wealthy hardware merchant Moses Gill (1733–1800) of Boston and Princeton, Massachusetts. The concertina-action card table, notable for its asymmetrical knee carving and gadrooned molding, is thought to have originally belonged to Capt. Thomas Frazar (ca. 1735–1782), a Scottish-born immigrant to Duxbury, Massachusetts. It descended to his grandson Amherst Alden Frazar (1804–1876) and later descendants before it too passed out of the family.

Attributed to Thomas Needham, Sr.
Boston, Mass., ca. 1780
Mahogany, white pine
H. 32 in., W. 36 1/2 in., D. 19 1/2 in.
Private collection

The bombé (or swelled) shape was used for high-style case furniture in Boston and Essex County in the second half of the 18th century, but it was not popular elsewhere in the colonies. Many of Boston's finest cabinetmakers, such as George Bright, Benjamin Frothingham, Thomas Sherburne, and John Cogswell, are known to have produced bombé furniture, and about 40 examples by various known and unknown Massachusetts makers have survived.

This chest of drawers, with a history in the Parkman and Scollay families, has recently been attributed to Thomas Needham, Sr. (1734–1804), a less well-known craftsman who worked in both Salem and Boston during his long and somewhat checkered career. A second closely related chest, also attributed to Needham, Sr., which shares many of the unusual construction details of this chest, was owned by Josiah Quincy.

Marble-top sideboard **25**
Attributed to John and Thomas Seymour
Boston, Mass., 1798–1810
Mahogany; mahogany, she-oak (*Casuarina*),
curly satinwood, and maple veneers; eastern
white pine, cherry, maple; marble
H. 33 in., W. 44 7/8 in., D. 21 7/8 in.
Private collection

Even though Massachusetts led the way in standing firm against the "insolent menaces of villains in power," as noted on Paul Revere's Sons of Liberty bowl, and attaining American political freedom from England, that drive for independence did not extend to the arts, which remained very much in the English tradition after the Revolution. In Boston the leading cabinetmakers in the federal period were the English-trained immigrants John Seymour (1738–1818) and his son Thomas (1771–1849). They produced stylish and costly neoclassical furniture for Boston patrons, but their hegemony extended outside the city to wealthy consumers in nearby towns. This elegant marble-topped sideboard, notable for (in the words of the Seymour scholar Robert D. Mussey, Jr.) being "the single finest example of inlay work on any known piece of Boston Federal furniture" and equal to any produced elsewhere in America, was made for John and Eleanor Derby of Salem. In good New England fashion, it has passed through many generations of the same family to the present owners.

26 Card table

Attributed to Thomas Seymour; carving attributed to Thomas Wightman

Boston, Mass., 1815-1820

Mahogany; mahogany and bird's-eye maple veneers; ash, chestnut

H. 30 in., W. 35 5/8 in., D. 18 3/8 in. (closed)

Private collection

Although somewhat difficult to decipher, a number inscribed in chalk on the rear rail of this card table may indicate that the original price for this table and its mate (now in the Winterthur Museum) was $235, an extraordinary sum for the time and indicative of the high quality of this tour de force of the cabinetmaker's art. Closely related to a pair valued at $200 and made by the Seymours at about the same time for *Cleopatra's Barge*, the luxury yacht owned by Salem merchant George Crowninshield, Jr., these tables were probably known as "harp-base" at the time. They contain many touches and details representative of the finest Boston work: a pierced brass and rosewood fretwork around the top, scorched maple veneers, imported English ormolu mounts, and carved scrolls and lyres by Thomas Wightman, an English immigrant who was the leading carver of his generation in Boston.

Marble-topped pier table **27**
Emmons and Archbald
Boston, Mass., 1813-1825
Mahogany, mahogany veneer, chestnut, pine, poplar, marble
H. 36 in., W. 29 1/4 in., D. 17 1/2 in.
Private collection

George Archbald, ca. 1840–1850

Pier tables were a staple of the Boston cabinetmaker's trade for several decades in the early 19th century, needed to furnish the many fine town houses being built in the city at that time. Few, however, are as beautiful as this small example, with its swooping curved rails at the front and sides, canted front corners with applied floral ornaments, and extraordinary front feet consisting of a well-articulated hairy-paw foot resting above a flattened-ball form. The underside of the original imported marble top contains an unusual marking that links it with Boston. A small diamond shape with a pellet or period in its center is thought to have been incised in the marble quarry to indicate that it had been ordered by a specific, although as yet unidentified, Boston merchant.

28 Secrétaire à abbatant

Isaac Vose and Son
Boston, Mass., 1819–1823
Mahogany, bay mahogany, eastern white pine, marble
H. 56 3/8 in., W. 39 1/8 in., D. 18 3/8 in.
Private collection

The focus of an ongoing research project by Robert D. Mussey, Jr., and Clark Pearce, Isaac Vose and Son was one of Boston's leading furniture shops in the years around 1820, creating stylish and sophisticated American expressions of the French empire style. This secrétaire à abbatant (fall-front desk), although unmarked, has been identified as the product of the Vose shop based on their identification of its many features diagnostic of Vose's fine workmanship, careful selection of veneers, and use of brass caps, bases, and applied mounts. Other Boston firms, notably Emmons and Archbald, produced similar secrétaires that share the same flat-top form and general sense of restrained elegance typical of Boston examples. The original marble top here provided an area for showcasing a clock, marble bust, or other precious objects. The applied mounts at the cornice, flanking a deep, blind document drawer, provide a fanciful depiction of a Native American at proper left and, at proper right, another female figure with a camel, who perhaps represents Asia, especially the Near and Middle East. The upper section of the desk interior contains shallow drawers, a row of pigeonholes, and a baize-lined surface for writing, while the lower case is fitted for adjustable bookshelves.

Dressing bureau with looking glass
Isaac Vose and Son
Boston, Mass., 1819–1823
Mahogany, mahogany veneer, ash,
yellow poplar, eastern white pine
H. 73 1/4 in., W. 43 1/4 in., D. 23 1/4 in.
Private collection

Cabinet 29
b
Attributed to Isaac Vose and Son
Boston, Mass., 1819–1823
Rosewood, mahogany, mahogany veneer,
yellow poplar, eastern white pine
H. 18 1/4 in., W. 18 3/4 in., D. 15 1/8 in.
Private collection

One large and one small, these two pieces demonstrate the high quality of the case furniture produced in the workshop of Isaac Vose and Son in the austere, late neoclassical style. The large dressing bureau with looking glass bears the firm's stenciled mark on the top of the upper drawer, and it is fashioned with the careful craftsmanship and enriched with the imported brass collars and pulls used to good effect by this sophisticated urban shop. The unmarked cabinet contains six shallow drawers on its interior; all but the top and bottom drawer are divided into one large and one smaller space with a side-to-side partition, and they do not show any other signs of interior fittings. It may have been designed to hold documents, coins and medals, or natural history specimens or for some other as-yet-unidentified purpose. It is distinguished by its fine veneers, the inlaid brass strip on its carved ribbed feet, and the menacing lion's-head carrying handles on the sides, all creating a masterpiece in miniature.

Side chair

Carved by Thomas Wightman
Boston, Mass., ca. 1820
Mahogany, birch, maple, ash
H. 33 1/4 in., W. 19 3/8 in., D. 20 1/4 in.
Private collection

Boston was the center of a large chairmaking trade in the late neoclassical period, and these two chairs embody just two of the many designs that were popular locally. Made in large sets for high-style Boston homes of the early 19th century, they have survived in quantities that belie their inherently fragile construction. Their saber legs are in the classic klismos form, and they clearly represent Bostonians' desire to embrace the classical style and all its affiliated virtues, qualities that they wished to associate with the new nation's culture and government. The back of one example (cat. no. 30a) features carved foliage and other elements attributed to the talented Thomas Wightman, while the other chair (cat. no. 30b), embellished with drapery swags in imitation of fabric, also has rope-carving flanking acanthus leafage on the front seat rail, triple-lobed anthemia on the crest rail, reeds, volutes, and other carved elements by an unidentified hand.

Side chair 30
Boston, Mass., 1815-1825 b
Mahogany, mahogany veneer, birch, maple
H. 33 in. W. 18 1/2 in., D. 20 3/4 in.
Private collection

31 Sofa

Isaac Vose and Son; upholstered by Otis Packard; carved by Thomas Wightman

Boston, Mass., 1823

Mahogany, sugar maple, cherry, with original underupholstery and modern show covers

H. 38 1/8 in., W. 76 in., D. 24 in.

The Colonial Society of Massachusetts; gift of the grandchildren of Francis Parkman

This large sofa, part of the Colonial Society's furnishings since about 1955, is a key piece in the study that Robert D. Mussey, Jr., and Clark Pearce are undertaking of Boston's late neoclassical furniture. Its significance lies in several areas in addition to its high visual quality and excellent condition. An inscription recently uncovered on the outside of the rear of the middle stile of the back reads, "Stuf'd by Otis Packard at / Isaac Vose's / Boston / August 24 1823 O P." In addition to providing the date and place of manufacture, this notation indicates that Packard, working as a journeyman or per-

haps as a subcontractor, "Stuf'd" (or upholstered) the sofa for the firm of Isaac Vose and Son, one of Boston's leading furniture makers in this period. A good deal of Packard's work on this piece survives, since the sofa retains much of its original underupholstery. Fragments of the original show covers also survive, and those small tufts and wisps guided the recent re-upholstery in peach-colored silk with green trim.

Stylistic analysis of the the excellent carving on the piece indicates that it is the work of Thomas Wightman (active 1802–1820), a

talented English-trained immigrant carver who had worked for John and Thomas Seymour. Thomas was the foreman in the Vose shop at the time this sofa—one of only a handful of examples to survive—was made.

The Colonial Society's records indicate that the sofa was given along with other objects by the grandchildren of the famous Boston historian Francis Parkman (1823–1893). It may have been owned originally by his parents, Rev. Francis Parkman and Caroline Hall Parkman, who were married in 1822.

Shelf clock **32**
Sawin and Dyar
Boston, Mass., 1822-1827
Mahogany, bay mahogany, eastern white pine
H. 31 in., W. 12 1/4 in., D. 5 1/4 in.
Private collection

This shelf clock was produced during the relatively brief Boston partnership of John Sawin (1799–1863) and George W. Dyar (1801–1871), in operation between 1822 and 1827 at 33 Market Street. Sawin had a strong link to the area's important community of 18th-century clockmakers in the Roxbury Village/Boston Neck area: he was the nephew of Aaron Willard and served an apprenticeship with Aaron Willard, Jr. After his training was completed, he joined forces with Dyar, and their firm produced a variety of timepieces for the next few years, after which the two young men separated and went their independent ways. The reverse-glass painting on the throat of this example was possibly executed by Charles Hubbard (1801–1875), an ornamental painter. Hubbard worked for Dyar after the Sawin and Dyar partnership dissolved in December 1827, and he may have been working for the firm earlier. The small temple, which sits at the top of this clock and supports the bell, strikes an appropriately classical finishing touch to the lyre-based form.

33
a
Side chair

Boston, Mass., ca. 1845-1850

Rosewood

H. 43 in., W. 18 in., D. 17 1/2 in.

Collection of Hilary Fairbanks and Timothy Burton

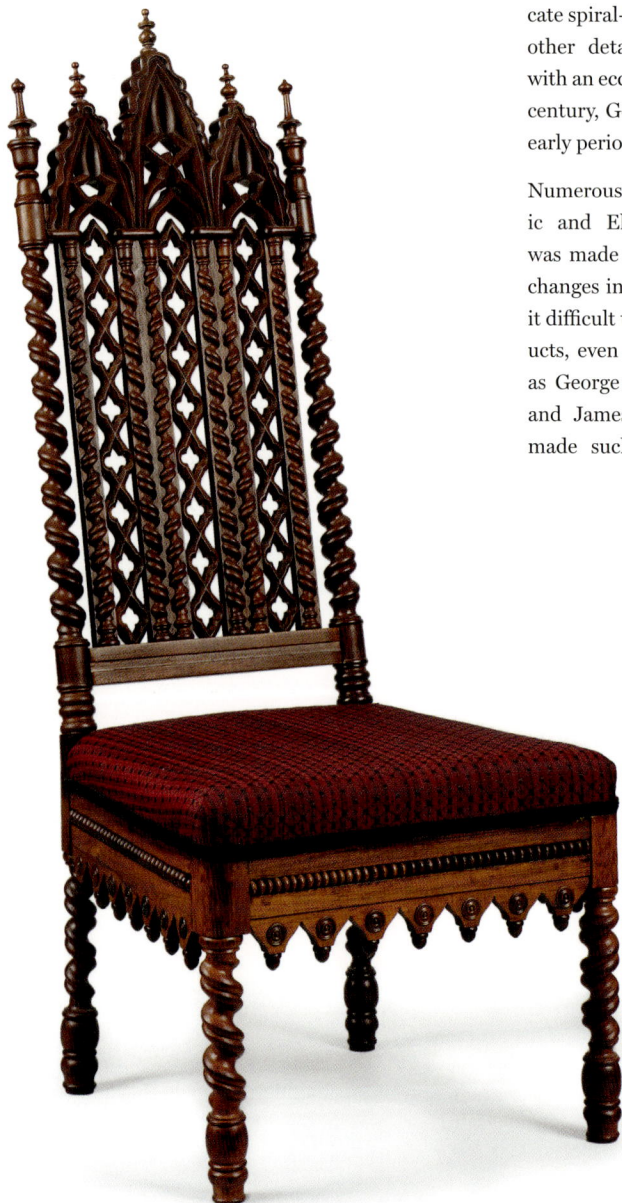

33
b
Stool

Boston, Mass., ca. 1845-1850

Mahogany

H. 11 in., W. 15 1/2 in., D. 15 1/2 in.

Collection of Hilary Fairbanks and Timothy Burton

These two objects feature the essential characteristics of the Gothic revival style. Based on the writings of the Englishman Augustus Welby North Pugin, this romantic style was introduced in America in the mid 1830s and became popular during the next decade. The pointed arch is perhaps its defining motif, often used in conjunction with pierced trefoils and quatrefoils, intricate spiral-turnings, applied bosses, and other details. While often associated with an ecclesiastical context later in the century, Gothic revival furniture of this early period was also used in the home.

Numerous sources indicate that Gothic and Elizabethan revival furniture was made in Boston by the 1840s, but changes in the furniture industry make it difficult to identify locally made products, even though Boston makers such as George Croome, Gilbert Whitmore, and James Paul advertised that they made such wares. One complicating factor is that furniture makers would import objects made elsewhere (New York, for example, a center of Gothic revival furniture) to sell at retail, but they would add their own label to the objects. The expansion of the retail trade, made possible by more efficient transportation and communication networks, exacerbates this difficulty, as the regional characteristics of furniture—relatively distinct in the 18th century—began to blur in the 19th.

These two objects were recovered locally, and it is likely that they were made in the Boston area. The side chair is notable for the delicacy of the carving on its triple-arched crest rail, for the crispness of its turned crockets and finials, and for the elaborate decorative scheme of its back, featuring applied twist or spiral turnings. The small stool features the arcaded skirt and applied bosses found on Boston-area pieces.

Table 34

Attributed to Edward Hennessey and Co. with
additional painted decoration by Annie Bigelow Lawrence
Boston, Mass., ca. 1846
Painted pine
H. 29 1/4 in., W. 34 1/4 in., D. 29 3/4 in.
Collection of Mr. and Mrs. Edward L. Stone

This Gothic revival table is part of a set of cottage furniture with a history of having been made by Edward Hennessey and Co. of Boston and embellished by Annie Bigelow Lawrence (1820–1893) in about 1846, the year of her marriage to Benjamin Smith Rotch (1817–1882) of New Bedford. The set consists of some 10 pieces of chamber furniture, painted overall in a cream or beige color and further decorated with gold striping and highlights. Lawrence added, as tradition records, polychrome floral decoration to the set and signed several of the pieces.

Edward Hennessey (act. ca. 1836–ca. 1859) was well known in the mid 19th century -as an important manufacturer of cottage furniture in Boston, but he is less well known today. A. J. Downing, in his influential *Architecture of Country Houses* (1850), praised Hennessey's moderate prices and extensive trade throughout the United States and West Indies, and the book illustrates two sets of chamber furniture (pp. 415–417). Downing observed that "some of the better sets have groups of flowers or other designs painted upon them with artistic skill"; Lawrence may have been attempting to emulate these factory designs. Hennessey flourished as a

maker of cottage furniture for a decade, but by the mid 1850s he shifted gears and operated a major multistory auction house on Winter Street. Downing's recommendation of Hennessey would have come to Lawrence's attention naturally. Henry Winthrop Sargent (1810–1882), her relative and a notable horticulturist and landscape gardener, supported the publication of Downing's book financially, and Downing in turn dedicated it to Sargent with his "sincere regard."

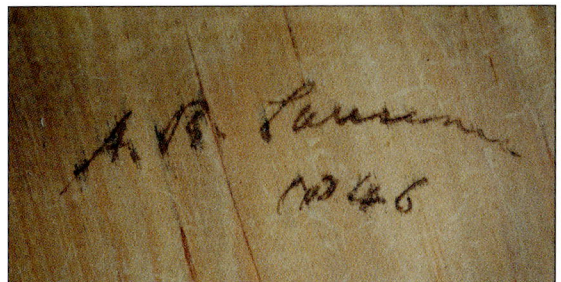

35 Library table

Probably Boston, Mass., ca. 1860

Walnut

H. 30 1/2 in., W. 57 in., D. 42 in.

L. Knife & Son Corporate Collection

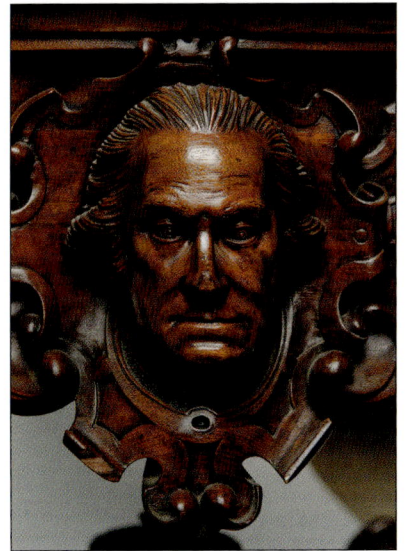

Large library tables of this type were a significant feature of many mid-19th-century interiors. This example was commissioned by Justin Winsor (1831–1897), man of letters, historian, and librarian of the Boston Public Library and Harvard. The work for which he is best known today is the four-volume *Memorial History of Boston*, published in 1880–1881 under his editorship, but his contributions to the professionalization of the library profession, to the history of the United States, and to many other fields are legion.

Born in Duxbury to a wealthy merchant and shipbroker, Winsor attended Harvard as a member of the class of 1853 but went off to Europe before graduating (he was granted the degree in 1868). After his return from his European sojourn, Winsor moved in with his parents in a new house on Blackstone Square in the South End, and he would remain there, even after his marriage in 1855, until 1880. Winsor carefully designed his library in that house, and this table occupied its center, surrounded with walls containing massive walnut bookcases, also embellished with figural carvings. Presumably the table traveled with the Winsors when they eventually moved to Cambridge in 1880.

The table itself is carved with busts, one to a side, of Washington, Franklin, Shakespeare, and Daniel Webster—"the soldier, the philosopher, the poet, and the statesman," as Winsor put it. It is in the rococo revival style of the mid 19th century, featuring cabriole legs, deeply carved C-scrolls and leafage, and scrolled cross-stretchers with a two-handled urn at their intersection. Winsor became a member of the Massachusetts Historical Society in 1877. After his death, his widow presented the table to the Society on October 15, 1900, where it joined his manuscripts and papers in the collection. The table resided with the MHS until it was deaccessioned in 1949. After passing through several hands, it is now in a distinguished local collection.

36 Miniature adjustable sofa

Augustus Eliaers

Boston, Mass., ca. 1850–1860

Walnut

H. 19 in., W. 42 in., D. 16 1/2 in.

Private collection

Augustus Eliaers, whose patent stamp appears at least twice on this small sofa, is best known today for his patented metamorphic chairs, which convert from seating furniture into library steps. This small sofa is also adjustable; after a brass catch at the rear is released, each end reclines to about a 45 degree angle, transforming a normal sofa to a more comfortable recliner. Eliaers (active in Boston from 1849 to 1865) patented a full-size adjustable lounge of very different form in 1853, and this little sofa may have been made at about that time. Elaiers, a French immigrant and a leading maker of rococo revival furniture in Boston, was clearly interested in innovative furniture, as were many craftsmen in the mid 19th century who experimented with new materials and created flexible forms that could serve multiple functions.

37 Side chair

Edward Hixon

Boston, Mass., 1857

Walnut

H. 41 3/4 in., W. 22 5/8 in., D. 22 1/2 in.

Massachusetts Historical Society

Boston, _April 7th_ 1857

Mass Historical Society

Bought of **EDWARD HIXON,**

Importer of Upholstery Goods, Trimmings, and Looking Glasses,
AND MANUFACTURER OF
CABINET FURNITURE OF THE LATEST STYLES & MOST THOROUGH WORKMANSHIP.
172 WASHINGTON STREET.

Transparent Shades,
BROCATELLE,
PLUSH,
SATIN DELAINE,
Gimps, Fringes,
Rope and Tassels,
Wholesale & Retail.

April 7th. 73 feet Bookcase Black Walnut
Carved finished in oil at
15.00 running foot — 1,095.00
1 Large Library table richly
Carved Marble top 70.00
16 Walnut Arm Chairs Covered
in Plush at 14.00 224.00
1 Walnut Mitre box also 1
Back Saw 3.00 $1,392.00

Recd Payt Edward Hixon
Apn 7/1857

The Massachusetts Historical Society purchased this rococo revival armchair on April 7, 1857, as part of the furnishings designed to house the library given to the MHS by the wealthy book collector Thomas Dowse. It is one of 16 walnut armchairs, covered in plush and valued at $14 each, specified on an itemized invoice from Edward Hixon, "Importer of Upholstery Goods, Trimmings, and Looking Glasses and Manufacturer of Cabinet Furniture of the Latest Styles & Most Thorough Workmanship" at 172 Washington Street, Boston. Hixon also provided 73 feet of carved black walnut bookcases at $15 per foot, a large library table "richly carved" for $70, and other items bringing the total to $1,392. Although he supplied furniture for Ogden Codman's house in Lincoln, Hixon's firm is not very well known today.

As the MHS evolved, Hixon's bookcases, table, and chairs were moved from their original setting to the Society's current home. They remain in daily use today.

38 Cradle

Boston, Mass., ca. 1863
Mahogany with rosewood graining
H. 62 in., W. 26 in., D. 46 1/2 in.
Collection of Mr. and Mrs. Francis L. Coolidge

In 1860 Isabella Stewart, later to become one of Boston's most famous personalities, married John L. ("Jack") Gardner, and the couple moved into their house at 152 Beacon Street. The couple's first and (as it would ensue) only child, John Lowell ("Jackie") Gardner III, was born on June 18, 1863, and spent his first days in this imposing cradle. Tragically, Jackie passed away from pneumonia on March 15, 1865. After a subsequent miscarriage, the Gardners, in a period of convalescence, traveled to Europe, a trip that stimulated their impressive collecting of European and Asian art that would, in time, lead to to-

day's Isabella Stewart Gardner Museum, one of the jewels in Boston's cultural life.

Jackie's cradle is in the rococo revival style, popular in Boston during the 1850s and 1860s. The open ribbed body, formed by bentwood slats and evocative of a ship's keel, is in keeping with the prescriptive advice of the period that air circulation was good for infants. The tall pole rising from one end terminates in a swan's head; a small bar in the swan's beak was used to suspend a drapery of mosquito netting or fabric.

Possibly designed by Henry Hobson Richardson
and his assistants at Gambrill & Richardson
Boston, Mass., ca. 1880
Oak
H. 60 1/2 in., W. 97 3/4 in., D. 22 in.
Massachusetts Historical Society

This richly carved, monumental piece of library furniture was made for Robert Treat Paine (1835–1910), a lawyer, social reformer, and philanthropist of Boston. Inscribed "Wisdom is better than Rubies" (Proverbs 8:11) on its doors and profusely embellished with carving and intricate brass mounts, it may have been designed by the noted architect Henry Hobson Richardson (1838–1886), with whom Paine had a close association. Paine was the head of the building committee for Trinity Church in Copley Square, Richardson's masterpiece, and the architect also designed Stonehurst, Paine's country estate in Waltham, completed in 1886.

An early photograph shows this cabinet in situ in Paine's city house at 6 Joy Street, with a gallery (now lost) around its top. A typed inventory of Paine's estate taken in 1911 indicates that the "Rubies" bookcase was located in the back parlor and valued at $75. An enigmatic ink annotation to that inventory gives the date "1880"and "H.H.R. 80" and "Norcross 800" above the line for the bookcase. Norcross Brothers served as Richardson's general contractor, but the architect also made use of other firms for furniture commissions, including D. Shales and Company Parlor Furniture Manufactory, Osborn's Mill, and Roeth and May.

40 Turned chair

Attributed to A.H. Davenport & Co.; possibly designed by Francis H. Bacon

Boston, Mass., ca. 1885-1895

Oak

H. 63 in., W. 41 in., D. 22 in.

Collection of Stephen Judge and James Skelton

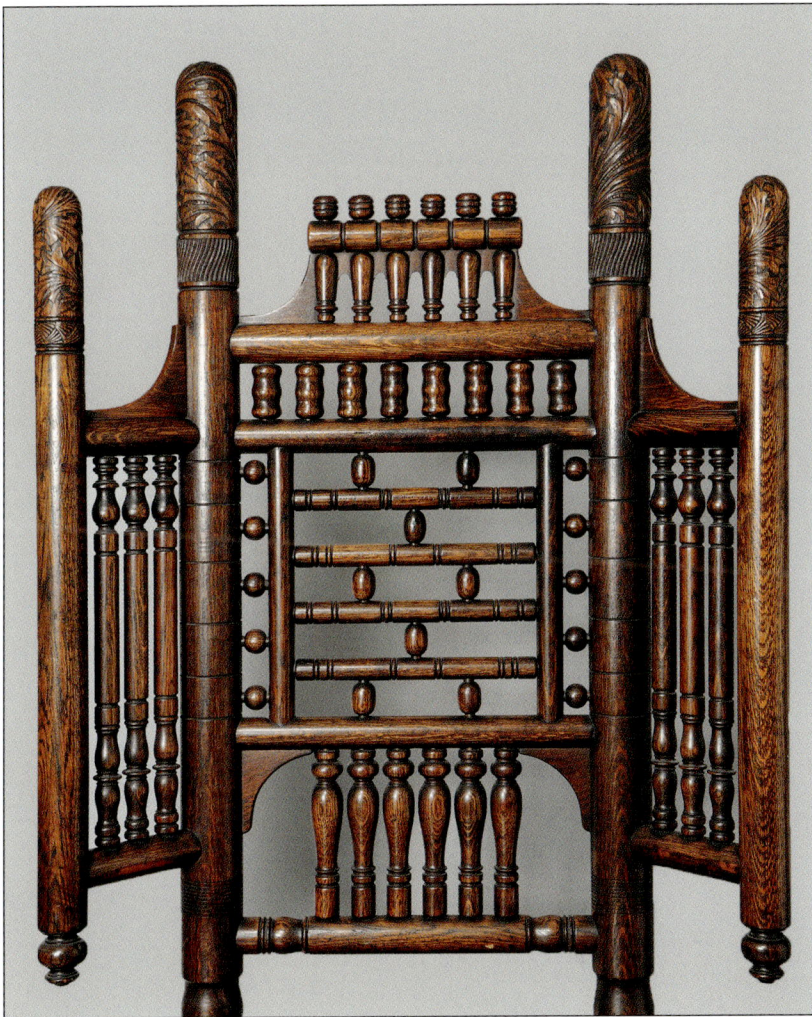

Monumental in stance, this imposing chair is a symphony of rings, reels, balusters, and spindles, a true homage to the art of the 17th-century turner. Although related to early American chairs, it more closely resembles elaborate English chairs of the period, which occasionally have the wing-pieces above the seat as seen here. In good revival-style fashion, the maker of this chair added carving to the top of the vertical posts in the back, a detail not found on 17th-century chairs.

A working drawing for a similar chair exists in a large archive of drawings now at the Museum of Fine Arts, Boston, from the Irving and Casson—A. H. Davenport and Company. This image and the style of the chair suggest that it may have been made by A. H. Davenport, a leading Boston firm of national significance. Francis H. Bacon (1856–1940), who remains little known, was Davenport's chief designer and may have been responsible for this chair.

An old photograph (Historic New England) shows this chair in the stair hall of an unknown home, presumably located in Boston. Collected locally about 30 years ago, this chair is today one of the highlights of the arts and crafts movement in Boston, reflecting the historicism and fine craftsmanship that are integral parts of that movement in New England.

A Note on Sources

The brief commentaries in this catalogue are based on a wide range of sources, including information provided by our knowledgeable lenders and the published work of many scholars. To date, the only book devoted solely to Boston furniture (not including monographs on individual makers, such as Robert D. Mussey, Jr.'s magnificent work on the Seymours) is the report of a 1972 conference held by the Colonial Society of Massachusetts and the Museum of Fine Arts, Boston, published as Walter Muir Whitehill, Jonathan L. Fairbanks, and Brock Jobe, eds., *Boston Furniture of the Eighteenth Century* (Charlottesville: University Press of Virginia, 1974). The essays and bibliography in that volume remain an important starting point for any study of Boston furniture. The MFA and CSM also published a small pamphlet to accompany a related exhibition entitled "A Bit of Vanity: Furniture of Eighteenth-Century Boston," held at the museum from May 11 to June 19, 1972.

Many articles key to this catalogue and to the modern study of Boston furniture as a whole have been published in the last twenty years in *American Furniture*, the journal edited by Luke Beckerdite and issued by the Chipstone Foundation of Milwaukee annually since 1993. Those important articles, as well as other works on Boston objects and on Massachusetts furniture as a whole, are listed in the bibliography I compiled for the Four Centuries of Massachusetts Furniture website (www.fourcenturies.org). Each issue of *American Furniture* also contains a bibliography of recent writing on all aspects of American furniture.

In addition, many of the papers delivered at the Winterthur Furniture Forum in March 2013 titled "New Perspectives on Boston Furniture, 1630–1860" provided fresh material on the types of objects included here and influenced the selection of objects for this exhibition. The conference speakers have been universally generous in sharing information about their ongoing research. Brock Jobe and I are currently editing those presentations for eventual publication in book form by the Colonial Society of Massachusetts.

The Massachusetts Historical Society acknowledges with gratitude the contributions of the following supporters of the Four Centuries of Massachusetts Furniture project whose gifts have made our exhibition and publication possible.

The Americana Foundation

Anonymous

Mr. and Mrs. James P. Barrow

Laura Beach and Joshua Kalkstein

Mr. and Mrs. Kenyon C. Bolton III

Anne and Peter Brooke

Margaret R. Burke and Dennis A. Fiori

Mrs. Elizabeth Campanella

Mr. Steven M. Champlin and
  Ms. Mary Beth Cahill

Mrs. I. W. Colburn

Wendy A. Cooper

Dr. and Mrs. Josef E. Fischer

Diane Garfield and Peter L. Gross, MD

Barbara and Robert Glauber

Mrs. Martha Hamilton

Ann and Donald Hare

Bill and Cile Hicks

Mr. and Mrs. James F. Hunnewell, Jr.

Brock W. Jobe

Mrs. Josiah K. Lilly

Jonathan B. Loring

The Lynch Foundation

Sara and Forbes Maner

Mr. and Mrs. G. Marshall Moriarty

Mr. and Mrs. L. Michael Moskovis

Robert and Elizabeth Owens

Nancy and George Putnam

Dr. Margaret B. and Mr. John C.
  Ruttenberg

Ruth P. Ryder

Ms. Sudie Schenck and
  Mr. Steve Goodwin

Mr. and Mrs. Roger T. Servison

Skinner, Inc.

Joseph Peter Spang

Gary R. Sullivan Antiques, Inc.

Jennifer and Matthew Thurlow

Mr. William W. Upton

Mr. and Mrs. Neil W. Wallace